rembrandt

rembrandt

Text by
SEAN KONECKY

LEON AMIEL • PUBLISHER
NEW YORK

Published by
LEON AMIEL • PUBLISHER
NEW YORK
ISBN 0-8148-0662-7
©Copyright 1977, by Leon Amiel • Publisher
Printed in the United States of America

Western civilization has witnessed very few
consummate artists. These are distinguished not
only by the fire of their genius but also by the
quality of their lives. The creation of a body of
work that renews itself with each new age
demands that the artist's courage and intensity
of vision be developed and sustained through a
lifetime. Perhaps Rembrandt, in the depth of his
commitment to life and in his capacity to trans-
mute this passion for humanity into the stuff of
art, is without rival. His life, as seen in retro-
spect, was a marvel of natural unfolding, in

which personal tragedy tempered youthful exuberance and faith transformed tragedy into wisdom and compassion.

Harmensz Rembrandt van Rijn was born in Leyden in 1606 of lower middle class parents. His father was a fairly well-to-do miller; his mother, the daughter of a baker. Rembrandt's time and place of birth were in many respects felicitous. His life span coincided with the high watermark of Dutch culture. Recalling Gray's flower, "born to blush unseen and waste its sweetness on the desert air," we can recognize that art is as much a cultural as an individual phenomenon.

The Seven United Provinces of the Netherlands had been engaged in bitter rebellion against the authority of Spain since late in the sixteenth century. A military truce signed in 1609 asserted the independence of the little Dutch nation. Its commercial interests and maritime strength were to give it hegemony in Europe for the next fifty years. Unlike the aristocratic monarchies of Spain, France and England, Holland's strength lay in its middle class. The vitality of the bourgeoisie, so amply documented in the paintings of Franz Hals, was the spur that impelled the Dutch nation to greatness.

The tone of life in Holland during the seventeenth century is best expressed in the works of its three great painters: Hals, Rembrandt and Vermeer. Hals drew the early stage of its cultural development. His subjects are somewhat

coarse, but they brim with life and self-confidence. Rembrandt's mature work represents the florescence of Dutch culture. His subjects are rooted to the soil; there is an acceptance of human nature. Yet we also see throughout Rembrandt's work an inner quality that reflects a society that has made a place for art and things of the mind. The decline of Rembrandt's popularity marks a third phase, the decline of Dutch supremacy. The painter of the hour is Vermeer. Vermeer is the epitome of refinement and subtle characterization, but his work speaks for a society that had somehow lost touch with the motive springs of its being.

In Rembrandt's early days, the title of burgher was a recommendation, not a handicap. Thus there was nothing unusual in his parents' encouraging him toward an academic career. At the age of 14, Rembrandt enrolled in the University of Leyden. Scholarly life, however, was not for him. Before long, his artistic inclinations won out and in 1621 he entered the workshop of the architectural painter Jacob van Swanenburgh as an apprentice.

Rembrandt's brief exposure to academia seems to have had little influence upon his life's work. His studies may have inspired his choice of certain mythological subjects, but what he learned there cannot be considered in any way formative. On the other hand, Rembrandt's work shows the influence and character of his parents. They communicated their devout religiosity to their son. From several of his early paintings we can see how Rembrandt was struck by his mother's sincere piety. Rembrandt's *Mother Reading the Bible* forecasts the shaping influence this peasant woman's religious conviction would have upon her son's life and work.

Rembrandt spent three years with van Swanenburgh. We can surmise that he acquired there a certain expertise and familiarity with painting convention, but there is no evidence that van Swanenburgh had any lasting influence on his pupil. At the end of his apprenticeship, Rembrandt went off to Amsterdam where he studied with Pieter Lastman. Lastman was a painter of some note, who excelled in the crowded canvas. He concentrated on Biblical and historical scenes, in which he emphasized the anec-

dotal or dramatic qualities of the action. He had incorporated in his work Dutch mannerism, and had acquired, by way of Elsheimer, the innovations of the Italian school. These influences he passed on to Rembrandt. Although Lastman's works are of historical importance, we look at them mainly because of our interest in his disciple. In themselves, they have little enduring value. Nonetheless, his paintings are skillfully composed and realistically depicted.

In this beginning stage of Rembrandt's career, Lastman's impact upon the young artist is evident. He, too, went in for flashy colors and tried to emulate the grand scale dramatic compositions of his master.

After six months in Amsterdam, Rembrandt returned to Leyden. He would remain there for the next six years. This was a period of experimentation. He devoted his energies to portraiture. His many self-portraits reflect not an inflated ego, but rather a determination to master the gamut of facial expression. For these studies, Rembrandt assumed a wide variety of emotional attitudes. This was, in a sense, preliminary work for a budding artist who wished to paint Biblical and mythical scenes in the Baroque tradition.

His genre studies of this period are especially interesting in that they show the waning of Lastman's influence. The artist's relation to his subject has become more intimate. Richly textured colors replace Lastman's surface brilliance. Rembrandt's choice of contemplatives for subjects surely corresponds to the intellectual atmosphere that surrounded him. The University of Leyden was celebrated as a place of learning.

One feature of Rembrandt's early work which is worthy of note is the sympathy and understanding with which he paints old people. Never before had a young artist shown so much empathy for the frailties and wisdom of old age. Read in the light of what was to come, these paintings seem to be groping toward a perception of inner qualities and a more complete experience.

Perhaps Rembrandt's finest work of this period is *Judas Returning the Thirty Pieces of Silver* (1629). Until recently it was only known in a number of copies. The original, however, seems to have turned up and is now in the Normanby Collection at Whitby. This painting marks a break with Lastman. In place of his teacher's bright, flat color, Rembrandt sought, through the use of chiaroscuro, a fluid rendering of space.

His treatment of Judas is highly suggestive. Dressed in rags, Judas kneels before the sumptuously attired Pharisees. They will have nothing to do with him. The light falls upon his face; it is convulsed with anguish and remorse. The silver, damning evidence of his treachery, lies scattered on the ground in front of him.

Rembrandt's ambitions in this painting overshot his developing abilities. He did not yet have the maturity to portray the self-horror of this most despised of men, and yet the boldness of

the attempt reveals much about the young artist. Here is expressed a breadth of compassion and an openness to human experience.

Rembrandt made quite a name for himself in Leyden. Constantine Huygens, secretary to the Prince of Orange, and himself a connoisseur of art, records a visit made to Rembrandt's studio. This was a high honor indeed to pay to one so young. Contemporary documents reveal that Rembrandt began taking on students at this time, another indication of his growing reputation. None of these would approach the stature of their teacher; one, however, Gerard Dou, developed into a miniaturist of some note.

The six years at Leyden were a period of germination for Rembrandt. All of his later concerns and most of his artistic motifs are present here in seed form. One notices his fledgling attempts at dramatic intensity (which he does achieve in *Judas*) and his contemplative bent. Though we might hesitate at calling any of these works great, they promise much.

In 1631, Rembrandt left Leyden for Amsterdam. This was an important step. He had gained enough self-confidence to strike out on his own. No doubt he was attracted by the wealth and sparkle of the city. No doubt his eye was upon the opportunities for commissions that a skillful portrait painter might obtain there. But his departure is best understood as a statement of personal growth. We can envision him taking leave of his parents, anxious to meet the world and test his own powers.

Before he left Leyden, Rembrandt established a connection with Heinrich van Uylensburgh, a successful Amsterdam art dealer. Upon his arrival in the capital, he took up residence with him. About this time, he painted *The Anatomy Lesson of Doctor Tulp*. There is some uncertainty as to whether he painted it right before or right after his departure from Leyden. At any rate, it marked a turning point in his career.

Rembrandt's unique handling of the subject becomes apparent by contrasting the painting to an earlier work, *The Anatomy Lesson of Dr. Van Der Neer*, by Michiel Miervelt. This latter painting does not go beyond a collection of individual portraits on a single canvas. The cadaver is downplayed so that it is little more than an insignia of the surgeon's craft.

Rembrandt's keen eye for portraiture is evident in his *Anatomy Lesson,* but he subordinates the individuals to the dramatic quality of the moment. His ordering of the canvas is fairly basic and shows the imprint of Lastman's compositional style. The lighting, however, is pure Rembrandt. Full light falls upon the lurid grey and yellow corpse. It is centrally positioned and captures the eye. Dr. Tulp conducts his exposition while the surgeons look on in concentration or stare at us with fixed intensity.

The painting was enthusiastically received and launched a string of successes that were to last for the next ten years. Rembrandt's way of life changed radically. He became the prodigy of the Amsterdam art world and enjoyed himself immensely. With the benefit of hindsight, we can recognize how this all-out encounter with the world contributed to the burgeoning of his creative powers. Some wonder at the ripe-

ness of later works, which were often painted at the brink of financial ruin or under the shadow of personal tragedy. But his later wisdom derives in part from his living out desires for personal wealth and fame. One finds little trace in his later works of the bitterness that speaks of chances missed.

During his meteoric rise, Rembrandt married Saskia van Uylensburgh, cousin to his landlord. Saskia came from a prestigious family. She herself possessed a considerable fortune. She introduced Rembrandt into wealthy circles in Amsterdam. Rembrandt became wealthy and well-known.

He received more commissions than he could handle. His house became a gathering place for artists. It was crammed with students. Rembrandt was not one to drink lightly of this heady wine. Contemporary reports tell us that he frequented auctions, buying anything that could conceivably be of use in his studio.

It is not surprising that Rembrandt grew a bit dizzy with success. The air of prosperity in Amsterdam was infectious, and it is easily understood that a young provincial might fall under the sway of new sensations. Rosenberg says of this period in the artist's life: "His human and artistic development cannot be fully understood without considering the exuberance of his first decade in Amsterdam. This period played an essential part in the dynamic unfolding of his nature, which swung to extremes before finding its ultimate balance."

Rembrandt's artistic style paralleled the new life upon which he had embarked. He received many commissions and accommodated himself to the demands of contemporary taste. *The Blinding of Samson* (1636) is extremely vivid, but marred by its sensationalism. Yet we must remember that the graphic handling of brutality is in the mainstream of the Baroque tradition. Something deeper is stirring in Rembrandt's rendering of Delilah. He catches her turning for a last glance at her fallen lover, as she flees from the cave. Her eyes shine triumphantly, with a feverish glitter. Rembrandt's acuity at revealing what lies underneath the surface is starting to manifest itself, albeit within the context of Baroque dramatics.

Rembrandt also turned his hand to subjects taken from mythology. Perhaps the finest of these paintings is that of Danaë. Art historians disputed for a long time the subject and title of this work; some believed that it represented an Old Testament scene. The efforts of the distinguished Renaissance historian Edwin Panofsky, however, have established, with a high degree of certainty, that it depicts the coming of Zeus to Danaë.

Here the light descends from the uppermost part of the canvas, representing or heralding Zeus' descent in a shower of gold coins. Danaë's face is lit with joyous anticipation. Her hand is outstretched, greeting the falling light. The rounded contours of her body, her curious air of sensuality joined with serenity make her one of

Rembrandt's most appealing nudes. In the background is the figure of Cupid bound, which, following Panofsky, signifies Danaë's approaching confinement.

In 1632, the Prince of Orange commissioned Rembrandt to do a sequence on the Passion. Of particular interest are his *Erection of the Cross* and *Descent from the Cross*. The *Descent* is

quite remarkable. Rembrandt departed from tradition, painting the body of Christ in a wholly realistic fashion. It slumps inanimately, as the mourners struggle to take it down. Rembrandt repainted the *Descent* twenty years later. We will see how the contrast of these two works reflects his growth as an artist.

Rembrandt portrays himself in both the *Erection* and the *Descent*. In the former, he stands with the centurions, a perpetrator of the crime. In the latter, he is a mourner and shares the burden of suffering. Nothing could speak more eloquently for Rembrandt's profound religious devotion, for his consciousness of his own fallen nature and his desire to participate in the life of Christ.

Rembrandt's easy life lasted for about a decade. In 1639, he moved into a larger house; the outlay of capital and additional expenses strained his resources. Three years later, Saskia died. She had fallen ill giving birth to their only surviving son, Titus.

Meanwhile the art world of Amsterdam was becoming disenchanted with Rembrandt's work. Van Dyck was beginning to come into fashion and with him, a brighter, more naturalistic style of painting. Rembrandt's explorations in chiaroscuro put off many of his wealthy clients.

Saskia's death had added to the artist's financial woes. She left him only a small income. Weighed down by personal tragedy and accumulating debts, he abandoned many of his social contacts and pretensions. His art shows a corresponding privateness. It was as if personal suffering had deepened his artistic sensitivity. He turned away from the gaudy theatrics of the Baroque, which he had exemplified in *The Blinding of Samson*. In place of society gatherings, he took to long rambles through the less than fashionable quarters of Amsterdam and the surrounding countryside. There he found subjects for many lovely genre studies and landscapes.

In 1642, Rembrandt painted his most widely acclaimed work, *The Night Watch*. Oddly enough, the canvas has been misnamed. A careful cleaning actually reveals it as a daylight scene. The surface varnish had darkened over the years, producing the effect of night. This priceless work was vandalized in 1975. Through the combined efforts of the Dutch Government and the staff of the Rykamuseum the painting has been restored.

Commissioned to paint a life-sized portrait of one Captain Banning Cocq and his shooting company, Rembrandt chagrined his client with the finished work. In it, portraiture is subordinated to total artistic effect. In sheer complexity, it represents the culmination of Rembrandt's Baroque period, but in its dynamic intensity, it presages a new style and attitude toward painting. The figures surge toward the viewer; contrasted red and yellow bring out fully the sense of movement. The captain is the pivot of the composition. Dressed in black, he is pushed to the fore by the color surrounding him.

Dramatically, he acts as a stillpoint, a source of direction in the tumult of human activity.

Modern critics have pointed out the limitations of *The Night Watch*. This criticism is, perhaps, directed more toward naive popular enthusiasm than the painting itself. In conception, size and complexity, it surpassed anything that the artist had heretofore attempted. It was in many ways experimental. Its realization required solutions to new technical problems. For instance, we notice that the painting resolves itself only when viewed from a distance. Up close, it is a conglomeration of highly pronounced details and wads of color. The spectator participates in the visual creation. He steps back and the pieces miraculously fall into place.

The Night Watch was the summation of long efforts at mastering, one might say recreating, the crowded dramatic canvas. In his portraiture of this period, we observe a process of simplification. The outer form of the subject yields to inner psychological depth. These paintings seem to be discoveries of the realness of his subjects.

Such is the case of the genre style portrait, *A Young Girl Leaning on a Window-Sill* (1645). The composition and use of chiaroscuro provide the impetus for a penetrating and intimate glimpse into her character. This psychological portraiture sets Rembrandt's works above the superficial paintings of his less inspired contemporaries.

Rembrandt invests his Biblical subjects with the same inwardness. They carry an almost pal-

pable fragrance of devotion. The Bible was profoundly meaningful to Rembrandt, an unparalleled inspiration in his work. I do not wish to give the impression, however, that his Biblical paintings were spiritual in the sense of transcendental or other-worldly. On the contrary, now comes into play a synthesis that illuminates his best work. His paintings are concerned with incarnation, the spirit clothed in human form. They are spiritual in that they communicate a real devotion, an accessible religion. Rem-

brandt directed his vision toward man and saw God there.

The Holy Family with Angels (1645) beautifully illustrates the artist's growth in treating religious themes. He had painted this same subject fifteen years before, about the time he moved to Amsterdam. The earlier work shows flamboyance, richness of color and sensuous form. His revision of the subject is greatly toned down. Subdued colors cast into prominence the light falling from an upper window onto the face

of the Christ child. The scene is in genre style. This simple unaffected approach emphasizes its inner content and communicates Rembrandt's faith in a God within rather than apart from human concerns.

Rembrandt also chose subjects from the Old Testament. His *Susanna and the Elders* (1647) is justly famous. The subject itself was, for a seventeenth century painter, a bit commonplace. Rembrandt had copied Lastman's painting of

Susanna in 1635. However, his later work differs significantly from the traditional handling of the subject.

Lastman, Rubens and others before them, conceived of the scene as a contrast between the sensuous vulnerability of the nude Susanna and the pawing lechery of the old men around her. Rembrandt's portrayal is of a different quality. His use of chiaroscuro obstructs our joining with the elders in viewing Susanna as a sexual object. Instead, in her helplessness, she becomes the object of our compassion. Her posture expressed the rigidity of a trapped animal, her eyes voice a mute appeal to our sensibilities.

In all of this, we see a shift away from the Baroque aesthetic; exuberance is restrained, sensational effects toned down. We are viewing a more mature art. The Baroque imposed dramatic significance on its subjects through striking color, a reliance on female voluptuousness, the balanced ordering of composition on a grand scale. Rembrandt's paintings assume the quality of a dialogue in which the painter's task is to reveal the inner life of his subjects.

Rembrandt lived quietly with his son Titus and a maidservant, Hendrickje Stoffels, who became the artist's model and mistress. Saskia had written into her will that if Rembrandt remarried, he would forfeit the small income he derived from her estate. Perhaps this explains why he and Hendrickje never married. Hendrickje was to suffer for this arrangement. She was called up before a church council and reprimanded for living in sin. Her love for Rembrandt must have been great to withstand this kind of social and religious pressure. On his side,

Rembrandt had a great warmth for this simple woman. His loving portraits of her testify to this. In 1654, she gave birth to their daughter Cornelia.

Rembrandt's financial situation deteriorated. In 1656, he asked the authorities for a *cessio bonorum* (seizure of goods) to avoid outright bankruptcy. His entire estate was sold at public auction. Rembrandt would remain a poor man for the rest of his life.

Although at this time Rembrandt's style of painting was not in vogue, he still received a number of commissions. There is good reason to believe that his reputation as a painter lasted

and that his exile from sophisticated art circles was to some extent self-imposed. The social climate in Holland was changing; tastes were becoming refined. The gap between rich and poor widened. It was said of Rembrandt: "In the autumn of his life (he) kept company mostly with common people and such as produced art."

Among his most notable paintings of the 1650's are *Jacob Blessing the Sons of Joseph* (1656), *The Descent from the Cross* (1651), *The Slaughtered Ox* (1655), and *Aristotle Contemplating the Bust of Homer* (1653).

Aristotle Contemplating the Bust of Homer is one of the greatest art treasures ever acquired by an American museum. It is presently in the permanent collection of the Metropolitan Museum in New York. The painting was bought for $2,300,000.

With a masterful use of color and chiaroscuro, Rembrandt conveys the meditative mood of the philosopher. His costume is white and black, with the gold of his chain highly pronounced on his black velvet robe. The whole picture is swathed in brown shadow. The subdued darkness is a counterpart of the philosopher's mind, which blazes into form like the chain around his neck.

Rembrandt painted *Jacob Blessing the Sons of Joseph* in 1656, a year marked by financial distress. Yet one would never know it from this painting. There is a solemnity of tone that raises it above purely human concerns. We are admitted to a ritual that has the power to exalt the actors and take them out of themselves. The transmission of the blessings of the patriarch is of significance to the Christian faith. Christ, we remember, is of the lineage of Jacob.

In this picture, Jacob outstretches his hand to give his blessing to the blond Ephraim. Joseph is somewhat perplexed, because according to tradition the old son, Manasseh, should receive the first, more potent blessing. Joseph respectfully tries to steer his father's hand to Manasseh, but Jacob will not be deterred. The Bible says of this: "He (Jacob) set Ephraim over Manasseh."

This work portrays the dialectic between the human and the divine. Joseph holds onto tradition, but Jacob is moved with prophetic intuition. While both figures can easily be interpreted in symbolic or allegorical terms, perhaps it is best just to look at the picture. It is within

time and in a sense about time (the passing of one generation to another), but there is something about this moment that seems archetypical and timeless.

Another fine religious painting of this period is the *Descent from the Cross*. Upon comparisons with his treatment of the same painting twenty years earlier, we can see how the artist's

orientation has turned inward. The earlier painting has obvious links with a work of Rubens, one
which Rembrandt knew from a copy. The body
of Christ is depicted with an almost shocking
realism. The dramatic quality of the scene
focuses the painting solidly in the Baroque.

His second picture is very different. The scope
of the canvas has narrowed. The open land-
scape of the first painting has been abandoned
in this composition. Our vision is brought to
bear exclusively on the group around the cross.

The picture focuses on the attenuated body of Christ, the face of the grief-stricken Nicodemus and the laborers who bear the body down. Mary's face forms a secondary center of light. All of the action takes place under the cover of pervading gloom.

For all its brilliant execution, the earlier Baroque painting is essentially static. In the second work, the mourners are drawn into a dynamic, flowing relationship with the body. The shroud ripples toward them; they are conduits of emotion which emanates from their central grief. We are struck by the vibrancy and energy of their feelings — captured by the artist at the source — which, spreading, would transform the world.

In 1655, Rembrandt painted *The Slaughtered Ox*, a chillingly graphic study. In choice of subject, it is not innovative. Beuckalaer, one of Curtsen's students, was the first to use it. Rembrandt's treatment, however, is unparalleled by anything until the time of Goya. A flayed ox

hangs suspended from a meat rack. The ox symbolically reveals a natural, fallen world, in which man must kill in order to survive.

In some ways the picture strikes us as extremely modern. It is reminiscent of Blake's *The Tyger*, which asks questions but provides no answers. Its concern is primarily ontological, with what is. Because of this, it has links with the concerns of many modern artists, whose messages become sublimated in a pure contemplation on form. Form becomes message. We can make of this painting what we wish. Rembrandt painted what he saw, an object occupying space.

Rembrandt's last years were lonely ones. In 1661, Hendrickje died. This must have been a severe blow to the aging artist. His deep affection for this peasant woman is manifest in many paintings for which she sat. Among these, the painting of Bathsheba has been most highly praised. Here, the winning intentness of Bathsheba's face rivals the beauty and sensuousness of her nude figure. Other paintings of Hendrickje include a series of portraits, painted over a ten-year period, and paintings of her as Flora and as Venus.

Times were hard for Rembrandt. His son, Titus, assumed the management of his finances, and although Rembrandt continued to be very productive, most of the proceeds from his work went to pay off debts. There is a somber cast to many of his later paintings; yet, these are his finest works. They show complete artistic

integrity; hardly a single brush stroke could be altered.

Many consider Rembrandt's greatest achievement to be *The Syndics of the Cloth Guild* (1662). Rembrandt represents the board of directors at a general meeting of the guild. The five directors (and the servant who stands behind them) face out toward their constituents. One has risen, perhaps in answer to some challenge from the floor, upsetting the static form of the composition, leaving it naturalistic and relaxed.

Rembrandt portrays the directors with close attention. Each is a distinct personality. The richness of color in the background, the gold and red of the table cloth, all complement the intensity of the individual portraits. Yet, the directors are dressed in plain black. The orderliness, even severity, of their costume speaks of the modulating and controlling power of the social ethos. Rembrandt presents us with a dialectic, the interchange between man and his social milieu. The coordination and balance in this painting intimate that the broadest scope for individual expression emerges out of the assumption of social responsibility.

The aged artist lived in seclusion. He had few visitors, and those who did come to see him found it difficult to pry him from the studio. In 1668 Titus died, only a few months after his marriage. Rembrandt was left alone with his young daughter Cornelia. He died at the age of 63 in October, 1669.

We have spoken of Rembrandt's quest to balance the sensual world of human experience with transcendental religious values. His art served to affirm their interrelatedness, showing the humanity of Christ and the divine spark within every man. In his final years, however, Rembrandt as artist became more detached, more introspective and less involved with human affairs. With the hindsight of the biographer, we see this last period as the completion of a wholly natural process of growth. Hendrickje's presence may have acted as ballast to the artist's thoughts. After her death, he turned more toward considerations of his own mortality and the afterlife.

The transcendental quality outweighs the personal in his last works. They are pure and universal. Man is elevated, allegorized. As a small part of a much greater reality, his highest function is to mirror the whole.

I would like to end this brief survey of Rembrandt's career with a few remarks on a self-portrait painted in 1659. Unlike Da Vinci or Rubens, Rembrandt left no written records. Yet his series of self-portraits, starting with those of his early days at Leyden, to his last in the year of his death, provide us with a sequential narrative of his developing artistic powers. At the same time, they form a kind of spiritual autobiography.

In many ways, the self-portrait of 1659 is his most impressive. The colors of his coat and mantle are muted, his dress devoid of orna-

ment. Nothing in the painting distracts us from his face. The shadows around the eyes suggest that light issues from an inner source. His facial expression reveals a strength and richness, tempered by suffering that in some way seems to be at one with the suffering of all men. Rembrandt looks out at us. In creating art, the artist has created himself.

Sean Konecky

LIST OF PLATES

PLATES

1
Self-Portrait
about 1628

2
Self-Portrait
1650

3
Balthazar's Feast
1635

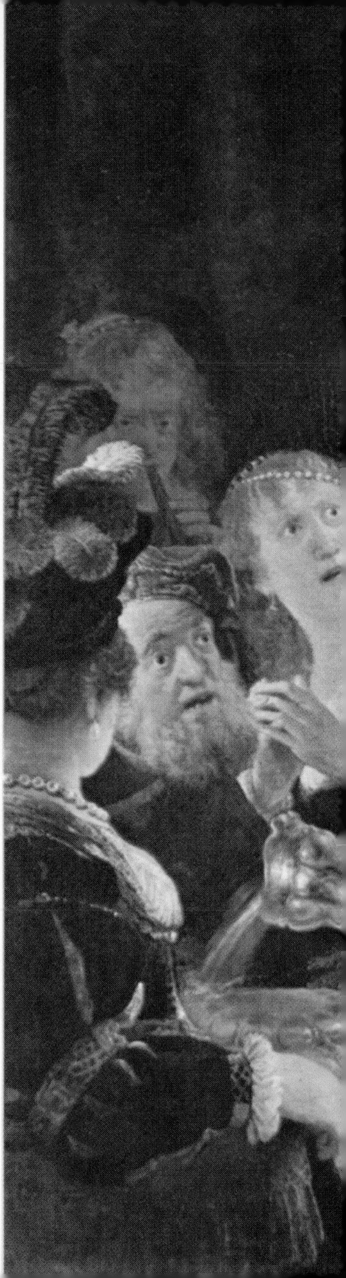

5
Balaam's Ass (detail)
1626

Judas Returning the
Thirty Pieces of Silver
1629

8
The Pilgrims from Emmaus
1648

Rembrandt's Mother (gravure)
1631

10
Rembrandt's Mother
Reading the Bible
1631

13
Head of Christ

14
The Descent from the Cross
1651

15
An Apostle in Prayer
1661

16
Saint Paul in Prison
1627

17
Self-Portrait
1659

18
Saskia Van Uilenburgh, the Wife of the Artist
1633

19
The Noble Slav
1632

20
A Polish Nobleman
1637

The Blinding of Samson
1636

24
Flight into Egypt
1627

Flight into Egypt: A Night Piece
1651

26
Pilate Washing Hands

27
The Presentation in the Temple
1631

28
Young Girl Leaning on a Window-Sill
1645

29
A Girl with a Broom
1651

30
Nicolaes Ruts
1631

31
A Turk
1630-35

32-33
The Night Watch
(ensemble and detail)
1642

34
Flora
1650

35
Lady with a Pink Flower

The Conspiracy of Claudius Civilis
1661

37
Philosopher in Meditation
1631

38
The Philosopher
1650

40
Monk Reading
1661

Portrait of a Lady with an Ostrich Feather Fan
1667

44
Saskia with a Red Flower
1641

45
Bathsheba
1654

Portrait of Hendrickje Stoffels
1652

47
Portrait of Hendrickje Stoffels
1658-59

48
Portrait of the Artist's Son, Titus
1650

49
Titus at a Writing Desk
1655

50
The Anatomy Lesson
of Dr. Nicholaes Tulp
1632

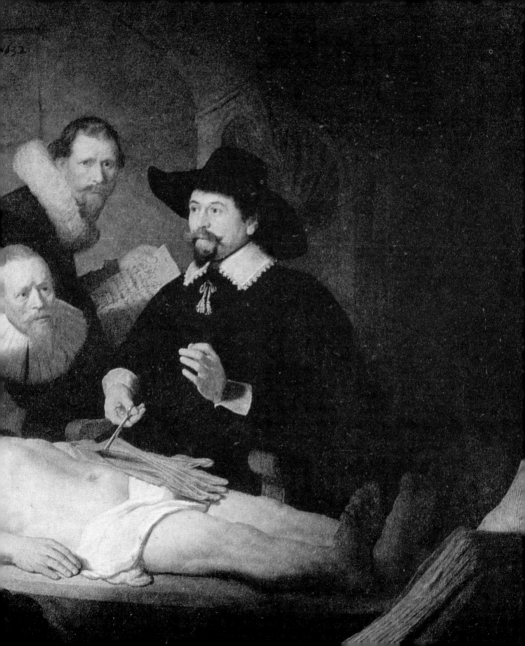

51
The Anatomy Lesson
of Dr. Joan Deyman
about 1656

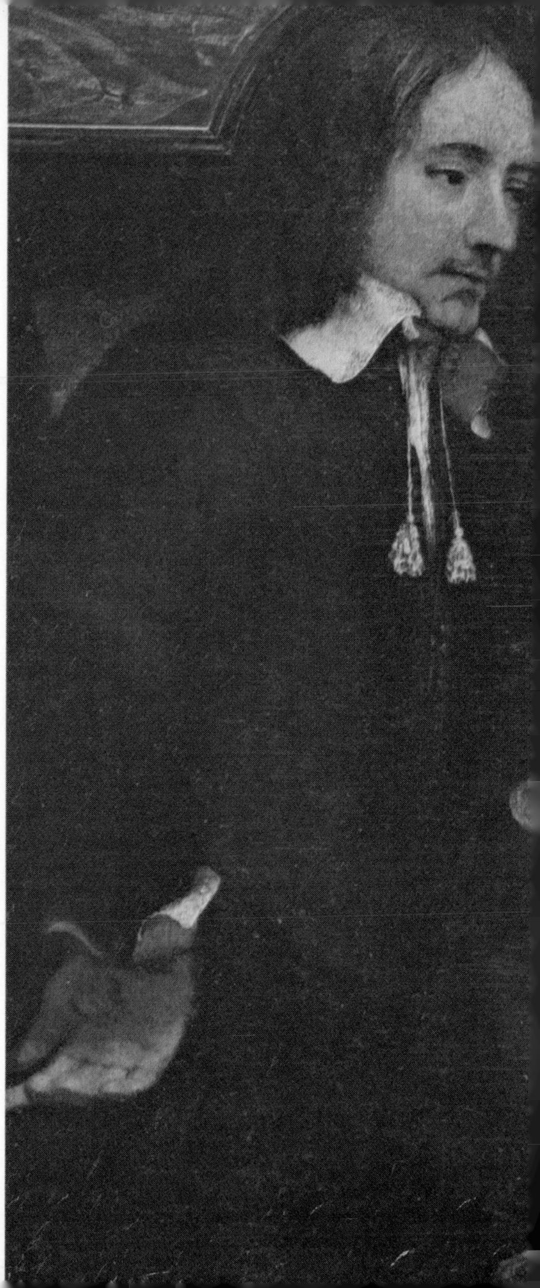

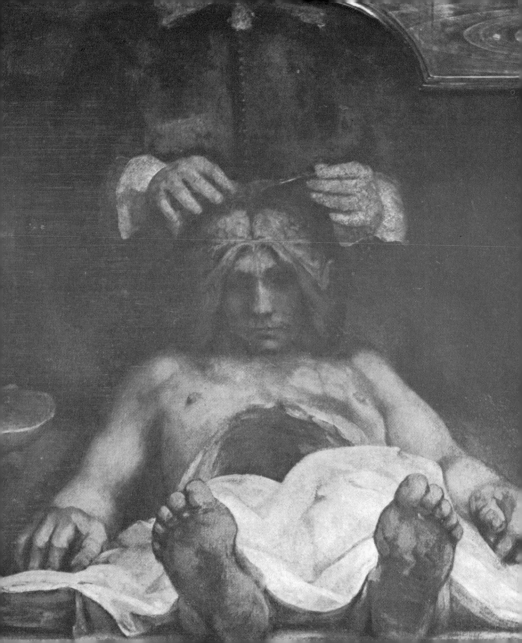

52
The Slaughtered Ox
1655

53
Self-Portrait with Bittern
1639

55-56
The Holy Family with Angels (ensemble and detail)
1645

57
Jacob Blessing the Sons
of Joseph
1656

59
David Harping before Saul
about 1657

58
David Taking Leave of Jonathan
1642

60
Susanna and the Elders
about 1641/1644

62
A Family Group
about 1668-69

64
Aristotle Contemplating Bust of Homer
1653

63
Juno
about 1665

65
The Jewish Bride
about 1665

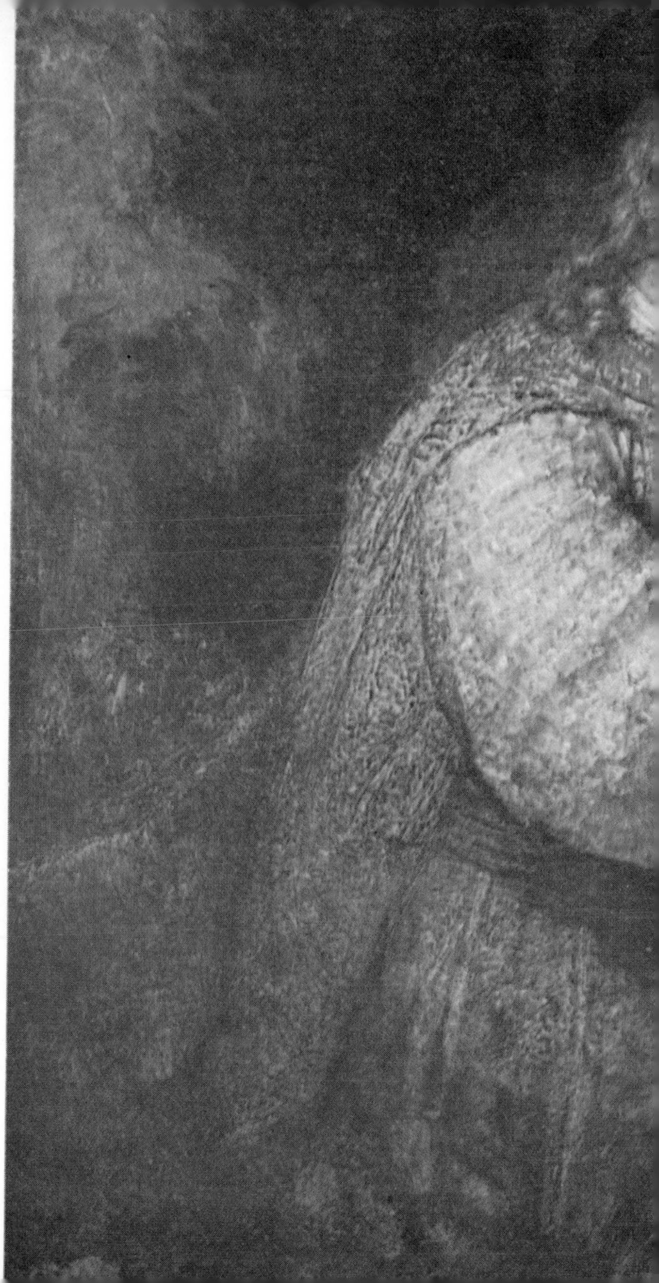

66
Lucretia
1664

67
Lucretia
1661

Rembrandt and Saskia at Table
about 1635